Improve your sight-reading!

Clarinet Grades 1–3

Paul Harris

NAME

EXAMINATION RECORD

Grade	Date	Mark

TEACHER'S NAME

TELEPHONE

First published in 1994 by Faber Music Ltd
Bloomsbury House 74–77 Great Russell Street London WC1B 3DA
Design and typography by James Butler
Music and text set by Silverfen
Cover illustration by Drew Hillier
Printed in England by Caligraving Ltd

ISBN10: 0-571-51464-2
EAN13: 978-0-571-51464-9

To buy Faber Music publications or to find out about the full range of titles available please contact your local music retailer or Faber Music sales enquiries:

Faber Music Limited, Burnt Mill, Elizabeth Way, Harlow, CM20 2HX England
Tel: +44 (0)1279 82 89 82 Fax: +44 (0)1279 82 89 83
sales@fabermusic.com fabermusic.com

INTRODUCTION

The ability to sight-read fluently is a most important part of your training as a clarinet player. Yet the *study* of sight-reading is often badly neglected by young players and is frequently regarded as no more than a rather unpleasant side-line. If you become a *good* sight-reader you will be able to learn pieces more quickly, and play in ensembles with confidence and assurance. Also, in grade examinations, good performance in the sight-reading test will result in useful extra marks!

Using the workbook

The purpose of this workbook is to incorporate sight-reading regularly into your practice and lessons, and to help you prepare for the sight-reading test in grade examinations. It offers you a progressive series of enjoyable and stimulating stages in which, with careful work, you should show considerable improvement from week to week.

Each stage consists of two parts: firstly, exercises which you should prepare in advance, along with a short piece with questions; and secondly, an unprepared test, to be found at the end of the book.

Your teacher will mark your work according to accuracy. Each stage carries a maximum of 50 marks and your work will be assessed as follows:

> 2 marks for each of the six questions relating to the prepared piece (total 12).
> 18 marks for the prepared piece itself.
> 20 marks for the unprepared test. (Teachers should devise a similar series of questions for the unprepared test, and take the answers into account when allocating a final mark.)

Space is given at the end of each stage for you to keep a running total of your marks as you progress. If you are scoring 40 or more each time you are doing well!

At the top of the first page in each stage you will see one or two new features to be introduced. There are then normally four different types of exercise:

1 **Rhythmic exercises** It is very important that you should be able to feel and maintain a steady beat. These exercises will help develop this ability. There are at least four ways of doing these exercises: clap or tap the lower line (the beat) while singing the upper line to 'la'; tap the lower line with your foot and clap the upper line; on a table or flat surface, tap the lower line with one hand and the upper line with the other; 'play' the lower line on a metronome and clap or tap the upper line.

2 **Melodic exercises** Fluent sight-reading depends on recognising melodic shapes at first glance. These shapes are often related to scales and arpeggios. Before you begin, always notice the *key-signature* and the notes affected by it, along with any accidentals.

3 **A prepared piece with questions** You should prepare carefully both the piece and the questions, which are to help you think about and understand the piece before you play it. Put your answers in the spaces provided.

4 **An unprepared piece** Finally, your teacher will give you an *unprepared* test to be read at *sight*. Make sure you have read the *Sight-reading Checklist* on page 23 before you begin each piece.

Remember to count throughout each piece and to keep going at a steady and even tempo. Always try to look ahead, at least to the next note or beat.

STAGE 1

C major

RHYTHMIC EXERCISES

1

2

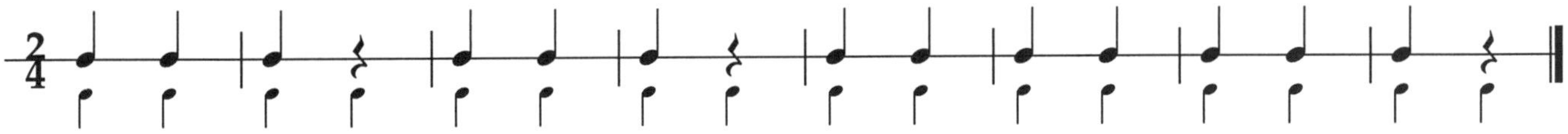

3

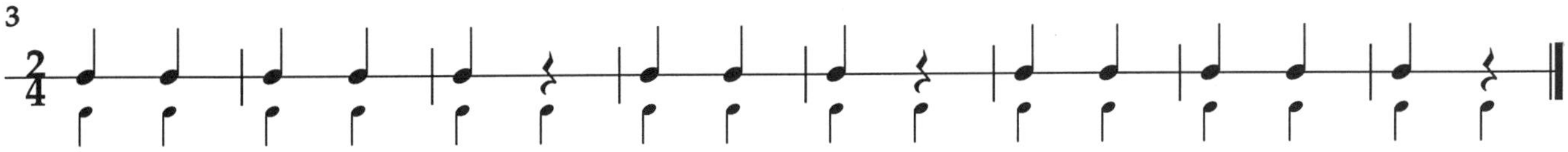

MELODIC EXERCISES

1

2

3

4

5

PREPARED PIECE

Marks*

1 What does *Moderato* mean? Medium speed ✓ ☐

2 What will you count? 2 ✓ ☐

3 What does ***mf*** (*mezzo-forte*) mean? quite loud ✓ ☐

4 What are the letter names of the first three notes? e f g ✓ ☐

5 What is the rest in bar two called? crotchet rest ✓ ☐

6 What is the duration of the rest? 1 ✓ ☐

Excellent! ☺

Total: ☐

Unprepared tests page 23

Mark: ☐

Prepared work total: ☐

Unprepared: ☐

Total: ☐

*The mark boxes are to be filled in by your teacher (see Introduction).

STAGE 2

9/6/14

Accidentals

RHYTHMIC EXERCISES

1

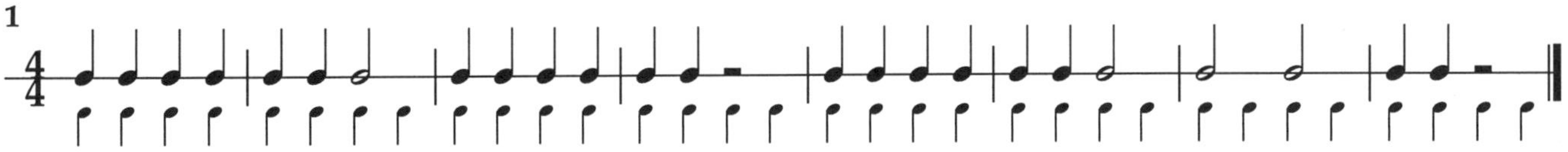

2

3

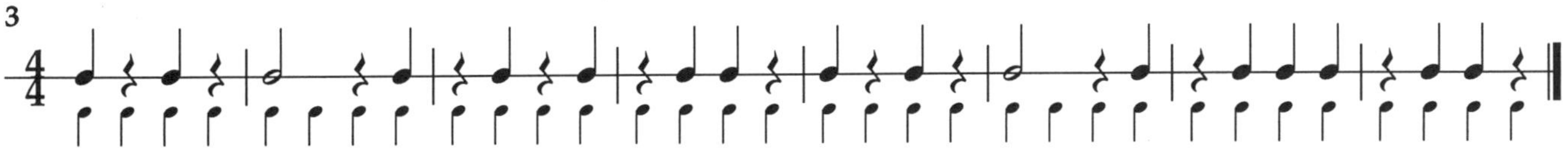

MELODIC EXERCISES

1

2

3

PREPARED PIECE 9/6/14

1 How many beats are there in each bar? 4

2 What are the letter names of the notes in bars 5 and 6? CDEGF#DGE

3 How many beats is each crotchet (♩) worth? 1

4 How many beats is each minim (𝅗𝅥) worth? 2

5 What does *Moderato* mean? Medium speed

6 What does *f (forte)* indicate? loud

Total:

Unprepared tests page 24

Mark:

Prepared work total:

Unprepared:

Total:

Running totals:

1	2

STAGE 3

9/6/14

3/4 F major

RHYTHMIC EXERCISES

1

2

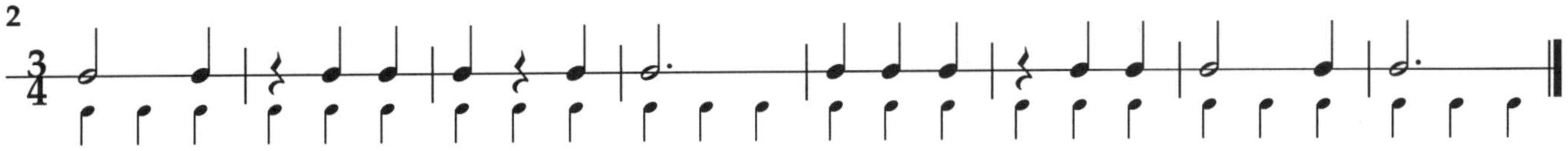

3

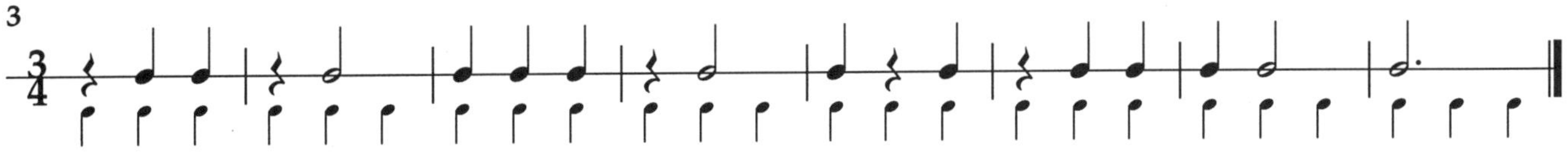

MELODIC EXERCISES

1

2

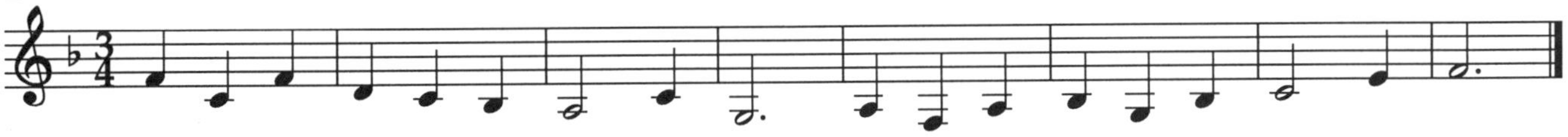

3

4

5

PREPARED PIECE 9/6/14

1 What does $\frac{3}{4}$ indicate?

2 How many beats is each minim (𝅗𝅥) worth?

3 How many beats is the dotted minim (𝅗𝅥.) worth?

4 What are the letter names of the notes in bar 13?

5 What does ***mf*** *(mezzo-forte)* indicate?

6 What is the meaning of *Andante*?

Total:

Unprepared tests page 25

Mark:

Prepared work total:

Unprepared:

Total:

Running totals:

1	2	3

STAGE 4

Slurs
G major

RHYTHMIC EXERCISES

1

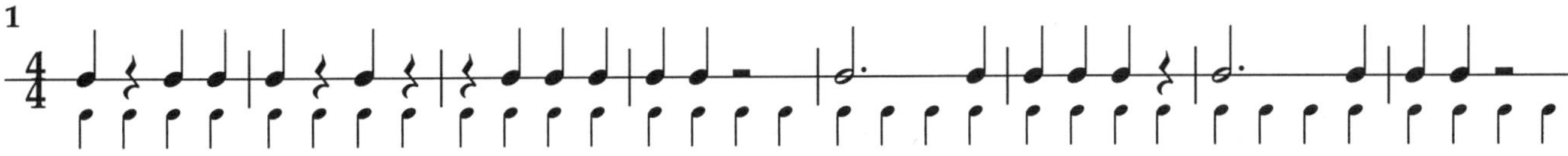

2

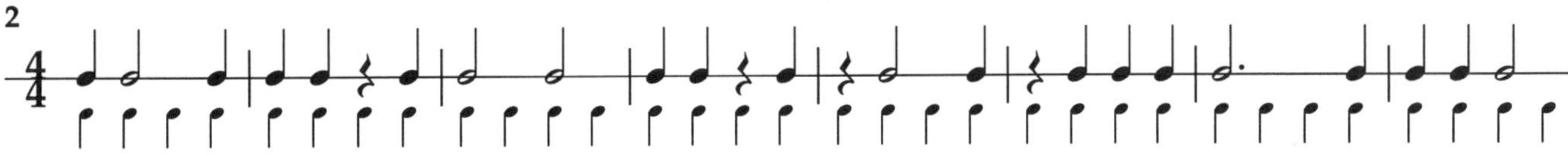

3

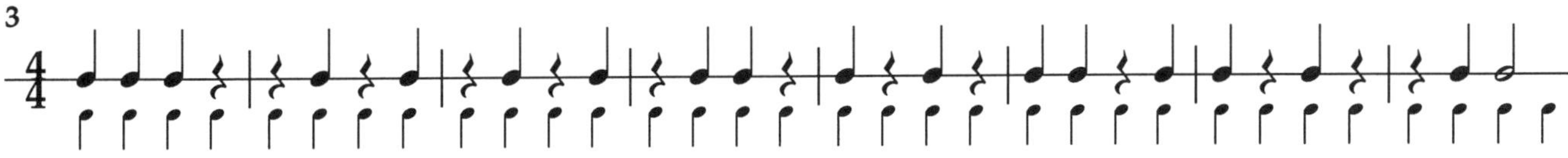

MELODIC EXERCISES

1

2

3

4

PREPARED PIECE

1 What is the function of a slur?

2 How many beats is each minim (𝅗𝅥) worth?

3 How many beats does this rest 𝄼 occupy?

4 What does ***p*** *(piano)* indicate?

5 What does < > indicate?

6 What is the meaning of *Allegretto*?

Total:

Unprepared tests page 26

Mark:

Prepared work total:

Unprepared:

Total:

Running totals:

1	2	3	4

STAGE 5

Staccato

RHYTHMIC EXERCISES

1

2

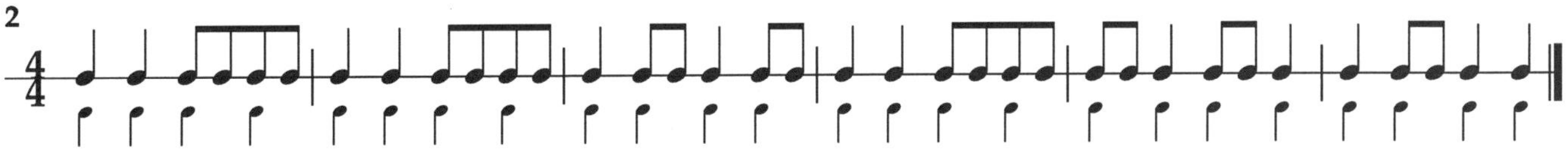

3

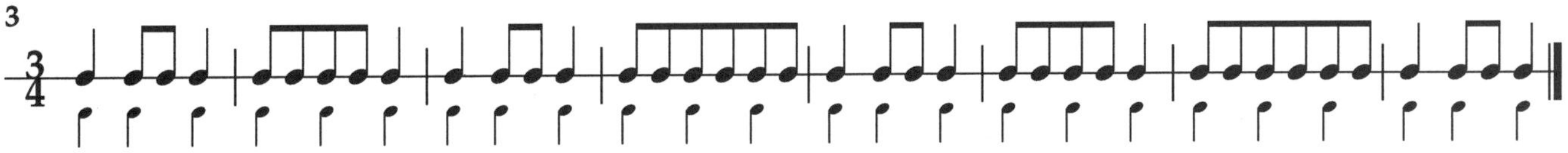

4

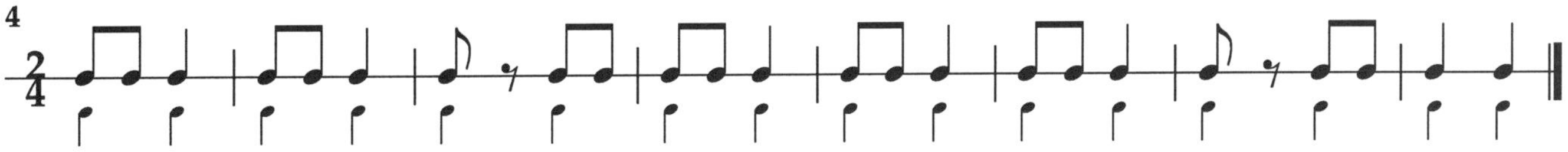

MELODIC EXERCISES

1

2

3

4

PREPARED PIECE

1 What does $\frac{4}{4}$ indicate? 4 beats in a bar

2 Clap the following rhythm: 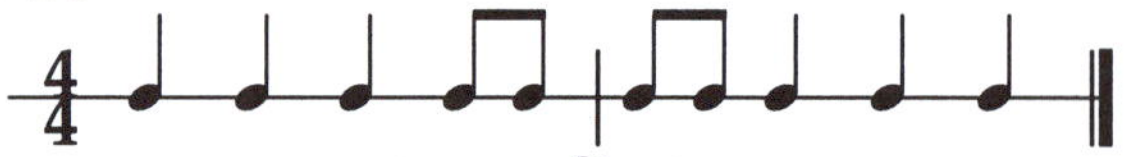

3 What do ***mf*** and ***p*** indicate? A quite loud B quiet

4 Which notes are affected by accidentals? F

5 What does ——— (*crescendo*) indicate? getting louder

6 What is the meaning of *Allegro moderato*? quite fast

Total:

Unprepared tests page 27

Mark:

Prepared work total:

Unprepared:

Total:

Running totals:

1	2	3	4	5

STAGE 6

23/9/14

A minor

RHYTHMIC EXERCISES

1

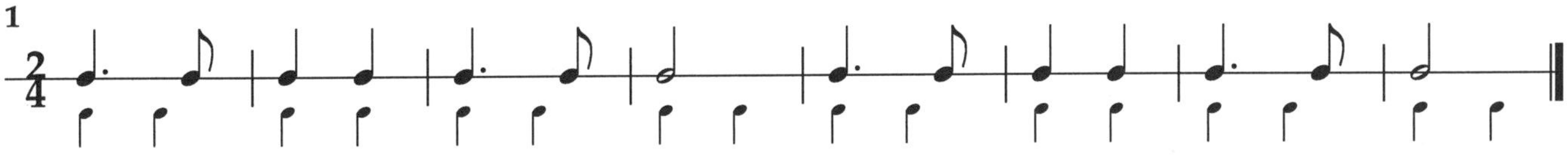

2

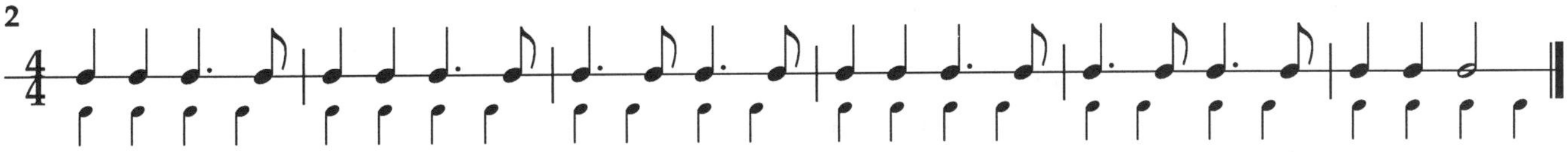

3

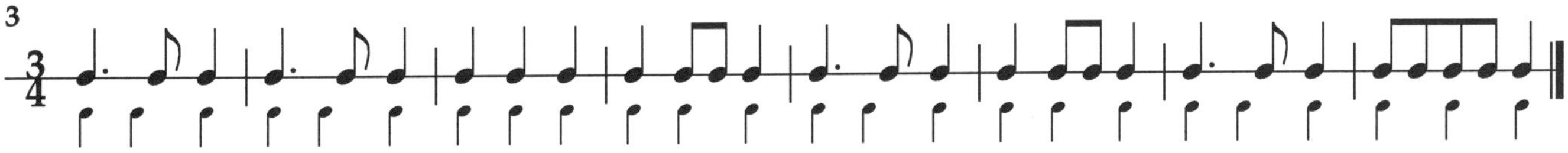

MELODIC EXERCISES

1

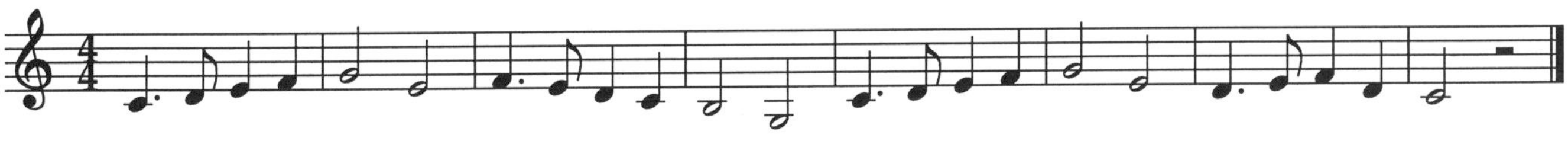

2

3

4

PREPARED PIECE 23/9/14

1 In which key is this piece written? C × A minor

2 Which of the following words best describe the character of this piece?
Flowing, Bold, Gentle, Angry, Jolly Flowerng

3 What do the dots under the notes (bar 7 and 9) mean? dotted rhythm

4 What does *rall. (rallentando)* indicate? ? Slow down

5 What does *Andante* mean? Middle speed ✓ Walking pace 2

6 Which form of the minor scale does this piece use? A Melodic

Total:

Unprepared tests page 28

Mark:

Prepared work total:

Unprepared:

Total:

Running totals:

1	2	3	4	5	6

STAGE 7

4/11/14

The upper register
D major
Simple tied notes

RHYTHMIC EXERCISES

1

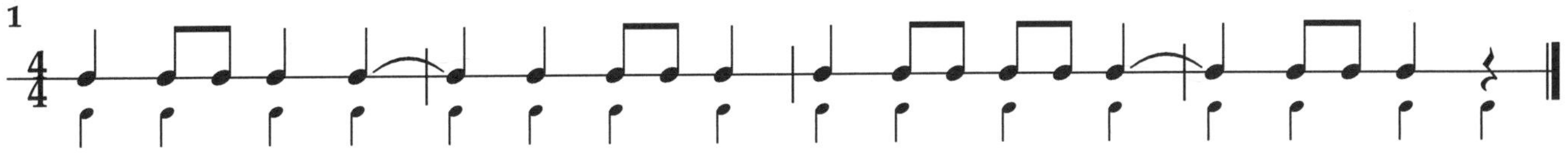

2

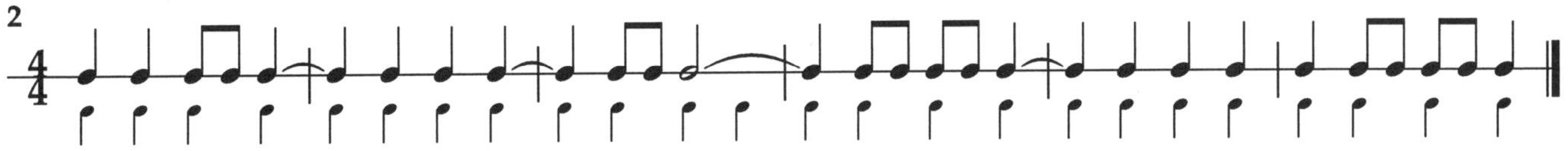

3

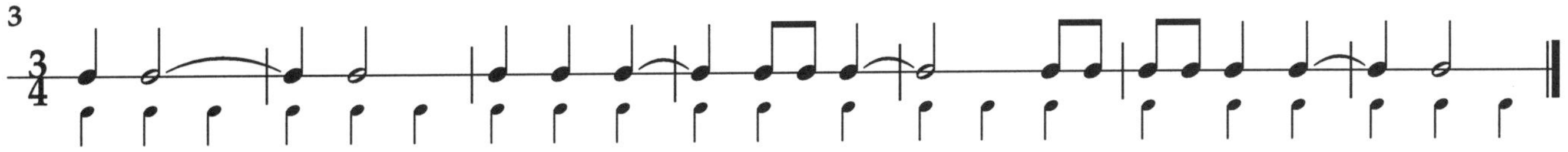

MELODIC EXERCISES

1

2

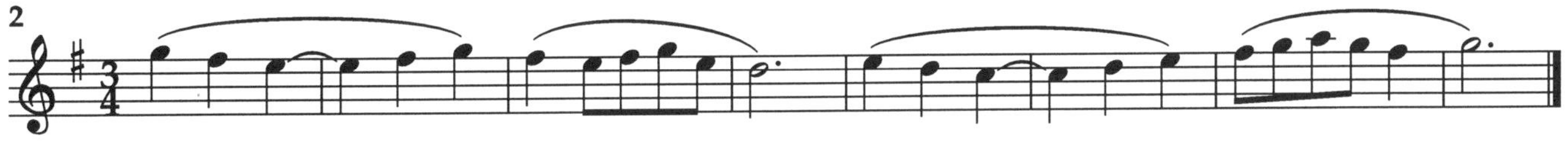

3

4

4/11/14

PREPARED PIECE

1 In which key is this piece written? A major

2 Which notes are affected by the key-signature? C♯ and F♯

3 How many beats are there in each bar? 4

4 What is the letter name of the first note in bar 4? bar 5? bar 6? E G F

5 What is the meaning of *Moderato con moto*? ?

6 Mark the tied notes with a cross.

Total:

Unprepared tests page 29

Mark:

Prepared work total:

Unprepared:

Total:

Running totals:

1	2	3	4	5	6	7

STAGE 8

19/5/15

Counting in quavers
$\frac{3}{8}$ B♭ major

RHYTHMIC EXERCISES

1

2

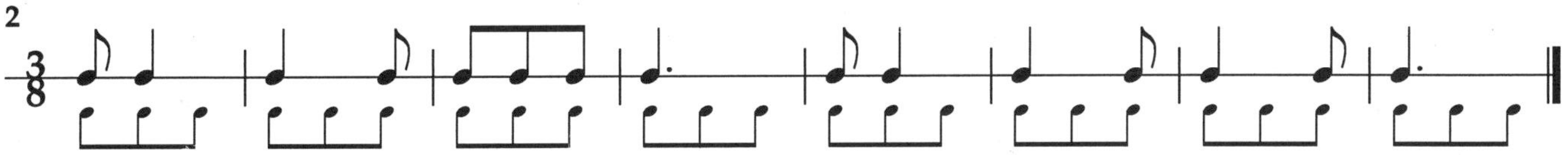

3

MELODIC EXERCISES

1

2

3

4

PREPARED PIECE

19/5/15

1 In which key is this piece written? B♭ major

2 What does *Allegretto con moto* mean? Quite lively with movement

3 What will you count? 3 quavers in a bar

4 What are the letter names of the notes in bars 3 and 15?

5 What does the articulation marking  indicate?

6 Which of the following words best describe the character and style of this piece?
Lighthearted, Tragic, Cantabile, Joyful

Total:

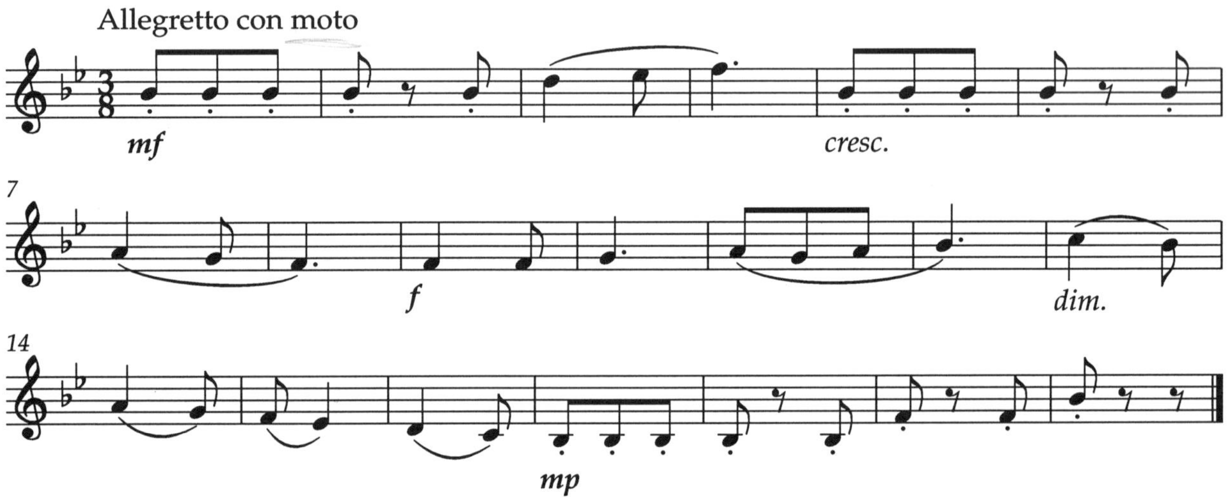

Unprepared tests page 30

Mark:

Prepared work total:

Unprepared:

Total:

Running totals:

1	2	3	4	5	6	7	8

STAGE 9

19/5/15 11/6/15

D minor

RHYTHMIC EXERCISES

1

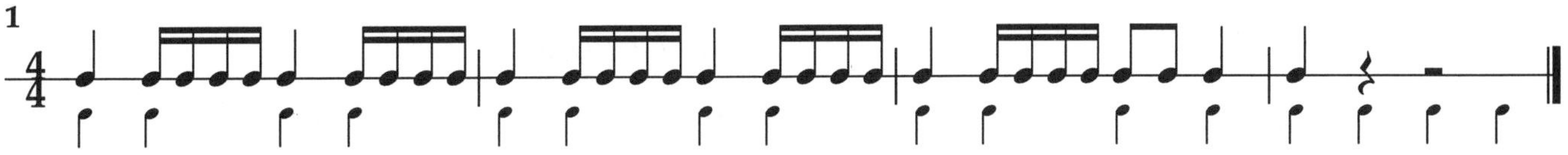

2

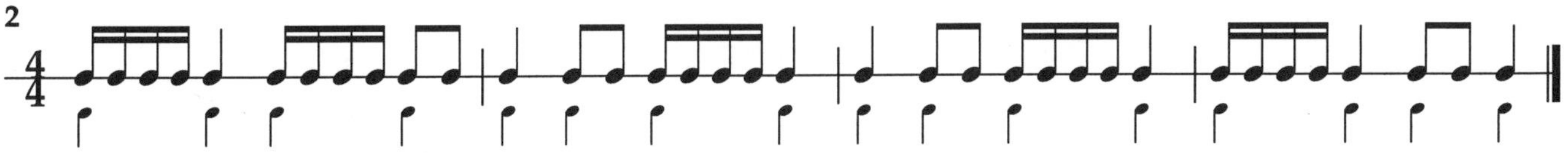

3

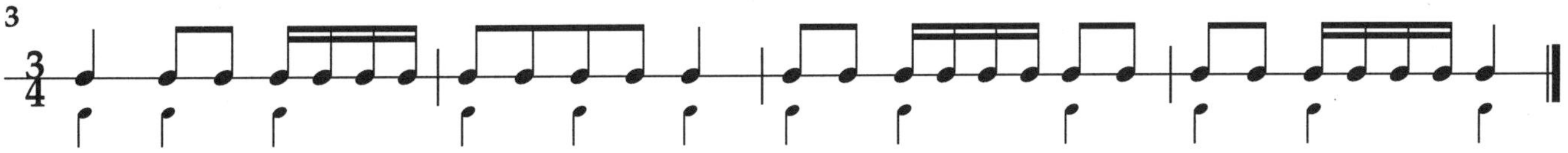

MELODIC EXERCISES

1

2

3

PREPARED PIECE 19/5/15 11/6/15

1 How many beats are there in each bar? 4

2 In which key is this piece written? F major D minor

3 Do you think this is a happy or a sad piece? Sad

4 Mark the first note affected by the key-signature. LOOK DOWN

5 What are the letter names of the notes in bar 4? EDC#

6 What does *rall. (rallentando)* indicate? Slow down

Total:

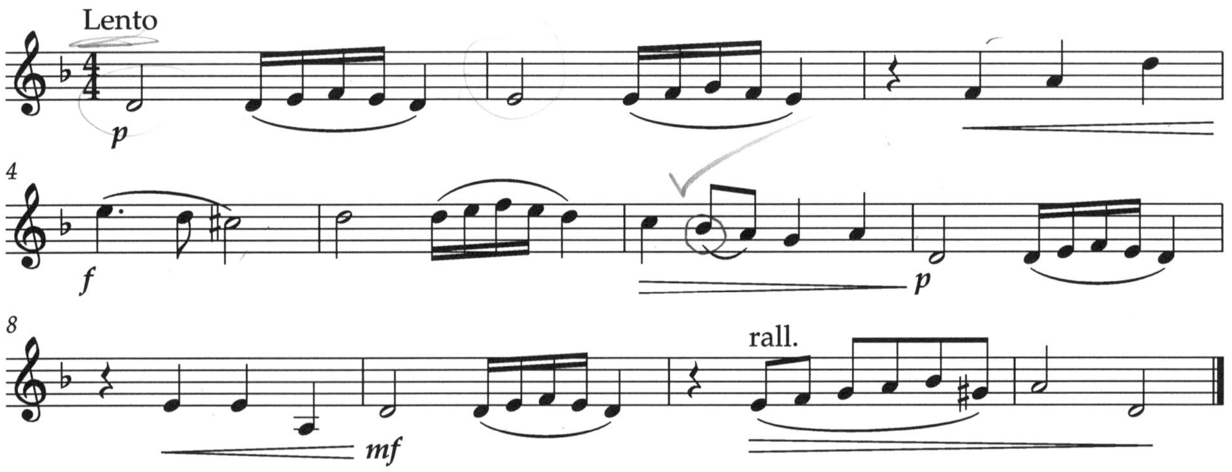

Unprepared tests page 31

Mark:

Prepared work total:

Unprepared:

Total:

Running totals:

1	2	3	4	5	6	7	8	9

STAGE 10

17/6/15

G minor

RHYTHMIC EXERCISES

1

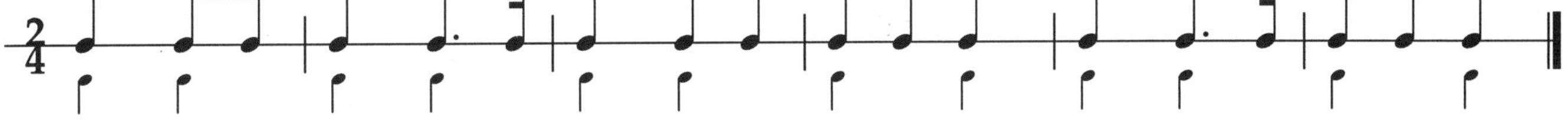

2

3

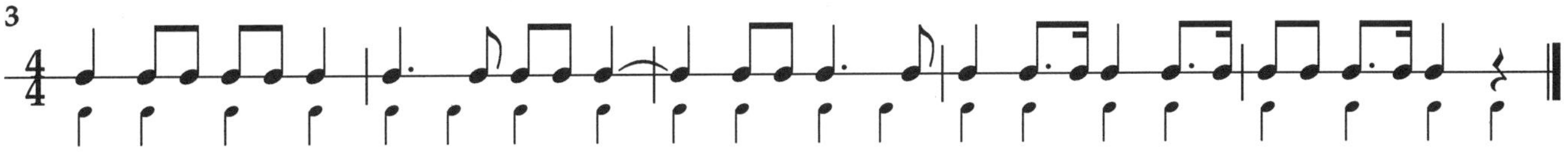

MELODIC EXERCISES

1

2

3

PREPARED PIECE 17/6/15

1 What are the clues that will help you identify the character of this piece?

2 How will you achieve a musical performance?

3 In which key is this piece written?

4 Mark with a bracket two bars in which the notes of the arpeggio of G major occur.

5 What does *Allegro giocoso* mean?

6 Clap this rhythm:  CLAPPED!

Total:

Unprepared tests page 32

Mark:

Prepared work total:

Unprepared:

Total:

Running totals:

1	2	3	4	5	6	7	8	9	10

UNPREPARED TESTS

A sight-reading checklist

Before you begin to play a piece at sight, always remember to consider the following:

1 Look at the key-signature, and find the notes which need raising or lowering.
2 Look at the time-signature, and decide how you will count the piece.
3 Notice any accidentals that may occur.
4 Notice scale and arpeggio patterns.
5 Work out leger-line notes if necessary.
6 Notice dynamic and other markings.
7 Look at the tempo mark and decide what speed to play.
8 Count one bar before you begin, to establish the speed.

When performing your sight-reading piece, always remember to:

1 CONTINUE TO COUNT THROUGHOUT THE PIECE.
2 Keep going at a steady and even tempo.
3 Ignore mistakes.
4 Check the key-signature at the beginning of each new line.
5 Look ahead – at least to the next beat or note.
6 Play *musically*.

STAGE 1

1 Allegretto

2 Moderato

3 Andante

STAGE 2

1 Moderato

2 Andante

3 Andante

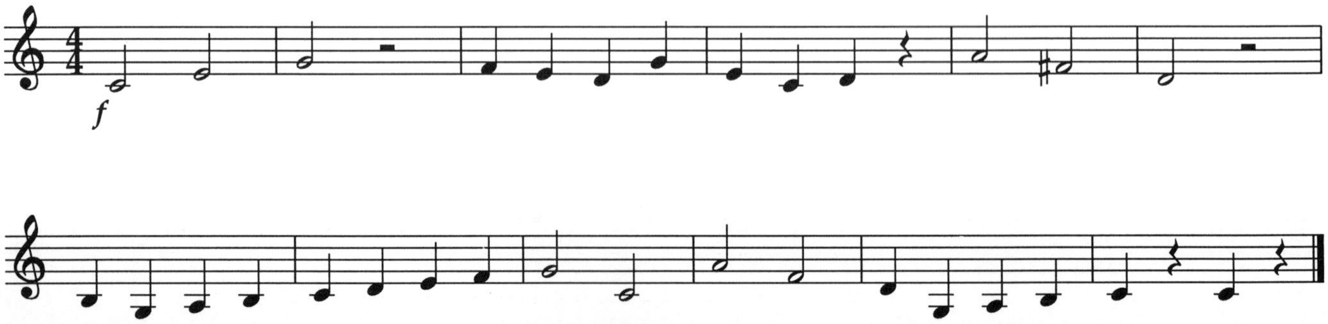

STAGE 3

1 Allegro moderato

2 Andante

3 Allegretto

STAGE 4

1 Moderato

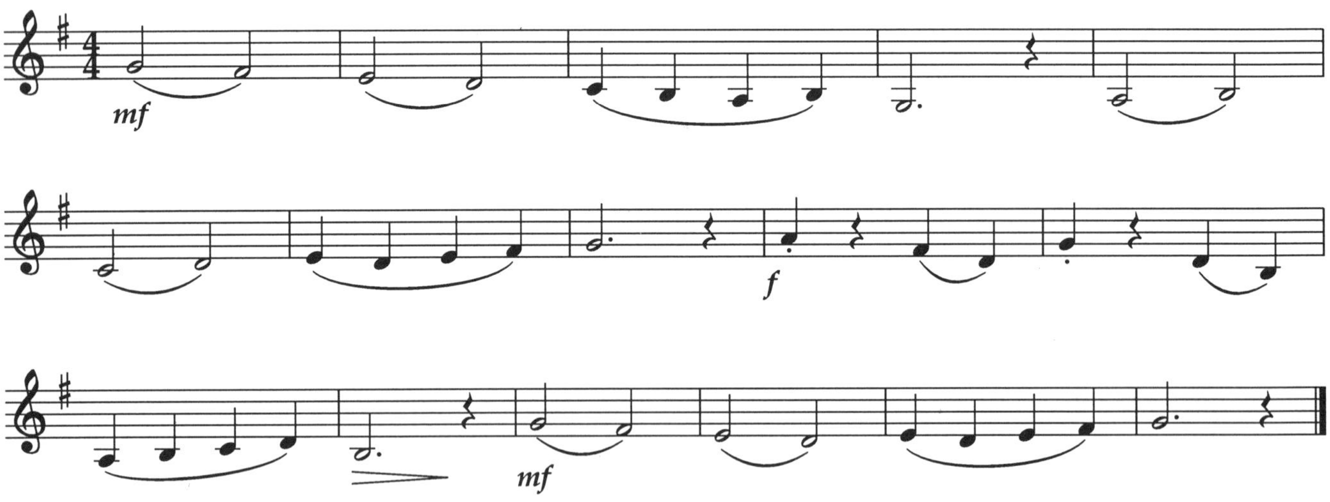

2 Allegretto

3 Moderato

STAGE 5

1 Andante con moto

2 Allegro moderato

3 Allegretto

STAGE 6

1 Moderato

2 Andantino

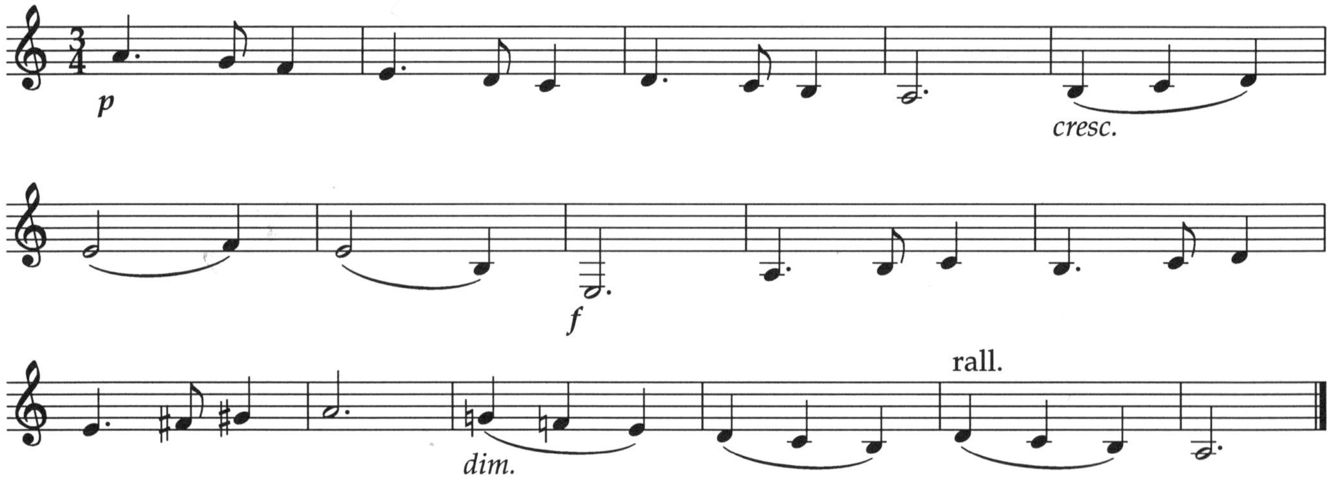

3 Allegretto

STAGE 7

1 Andante

2 Andantino

3 Adagio espressivo

STAGE 8

11/6/15

1 Andante

2 Animato

3 Risoluto

STAGE 9

1 Andante

2 Andante

3 Con moto

STAGE 10

1 Allegro

2 Andante con moto

3 Allegretto spiritoso